explaining

DOWN

SYNDROME

ANGELA ROYSTON

A⁺

Smart Apple Media

Smart Apple Media
P.O. Box 3263, Mankato, Minnesota 56002

Printed in the United States of America at
Corporate Graphics in North Mankato, Minnesota.

Published by arrangement with the Watts
Publishing Group Ltd, London.

Library of Congress Cataloging-in-Publication Data

Royston, Angela.
  Explaining down syndrome / Angela Royston.
      p. cm. – (Explaining–)
  Includes index.
  ISBN 978-1-59920-308-9 (hardcover)
  1. Down syndrome–Juvenile literature. I. Title.
  RJ506.D68R694 2010
  618.92'858842–dc22

                              2008049291

Planning and production by Discovery Books Limited
Managing Editor: Laura Durman
Editor: Annabel Savery
Designer: Keith Williams
Picture research: Rachel Tisdale
Consultants: Susannah Seyman and Stuart Mills,
  Down Syndrome Association.

9 8 7 6 5 4 3 2
32010
1205

Photo acknowledgements: Corbis: pp. 9 (Mika/Zefa), 19
(Mika/Zefa), 30 (Heidi Benser/Zefa), 33 (Tony
Gentile/Reuters), 36 (Mika/Zefa), 37(Mika/Zefa); Down
Syndrome Association: pp. 10, 11, 26, 29, 32;
istockphoto.com: pp. 15 (Huang Yao-Tsung), 25, 28 (Sylvia
Cook), 38 (Tomasz Markowski); Jackie Phillips: p. 35;
www.JohnBirdsall.co.uk: front cover top, front cover bottom
left, pp. 8, 20, 22, 24, 31, 34, 39; Library of Congress: p. 13;
Science Photo Library: front cover bottom right (LA LA), pp. 16,
(L. Williat/East Anglian Regional Genetics Services), 17, 23
(Saturn Stills), 27 (LA LA)

Source credits: We would like to thank the following for
their contribution:
National Geographic Society Kids Website,
http://kids.nationalgeographic.com/Stories/PeoplePlaces/Do
wnsyndrome; Sara Brownson,
http://www.centrecountydownsyndrome.org/personal_stories.
shtml#postnatal; Fiona Place

*Please note the case studies in this book are either true life
stories or based on true life stories.*

*The pictures in the book feature a mixture of adults
and children with and without Down syndrome. Some of the
photographs feature models, and it should not be implied
that they have Down syndrome.*

Contents

What is Down Syndrome?

Down syndrome is a genetic condition that affects about one in every 800 people. A genetic condition is something you are born with. You cannot catch Down syndrome from someone who has it and, if you have it, you cannot pass it on to your friends or to people you meet.

What Causes Down Syndrome?

People with Down syndrome have an extra chromosome (see pages 14-17). Most people have 46 chromosomes but people with Down syndrome have 47. The condition affects people in a number of different ways, including their appearance.

Effects of Down Syndrome

You can often tell that someone has Down syndrome from the way they look. Their faces are usually rounder and flatter than other people's, and their eyes may slant a little. The extra chromosome in their cells also affects how quickly they learn new things, causing them to learn more slowly than other children. Many people with Down syndrome have particular health problems, such as a heart problem or hearing loss. People who have another condition, such as autism or cerebral palsy, as well as Down syndrome may have more difficulties with learning.

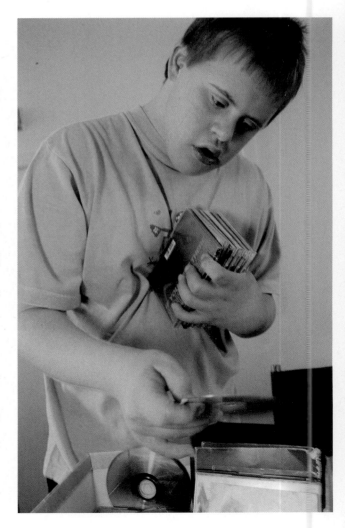

▶ *Like most young people, this boy enjoys listening to music from his collection of CDs.*

Same as Everyone Else

People with Down syndrome have the same basic needs as everyone else but they may also require additional support. Every person with Down syndrome is different and, with the necessary help, they can live the same kind of lives as everyone else.

▲ *Young people with and without Down syndrome can enjoy being together and learn a lot from each other.*

They can go to the same schools and enjoy the same things. Some people with Down syndrome leave home when they grow up and live independent lives.

Changing Attitudes

The attitude of people towards Down syndrome has changed greatly in the last 40 to 50 years. Before the 1950s and 1960s, people thought that children with the condition would never achieve very much and little was done to help them. Today, people understand that with support and extra input, children with Down syndrome can, and do, achieve a great deal.

Low Expectations

Many babies with Down syndrome have weak muscles and poor coordination. For this reason they take longer to make even simple movements, such as lifting their head, rolling over, and sitting up. In the past, and still in some countries today, people assumed that babies and children with Down syndrome would not learn and develop as other children do. Some people thought it was wrong to expect them to do what other children did, and so children with Down syndrome fell further and further behind.

Special Schools

In the past, children with Down syndrome did not go to mainstream schools. Some went to special schools, along with children with different disabilities. These children were separated from other children and not taught the same things. Some received no education at all. Families were often told that children with Down syndrome

▶ *In mainstream schools, children with Down syndrome take part in lessons and sporting activities with other children in their class.*

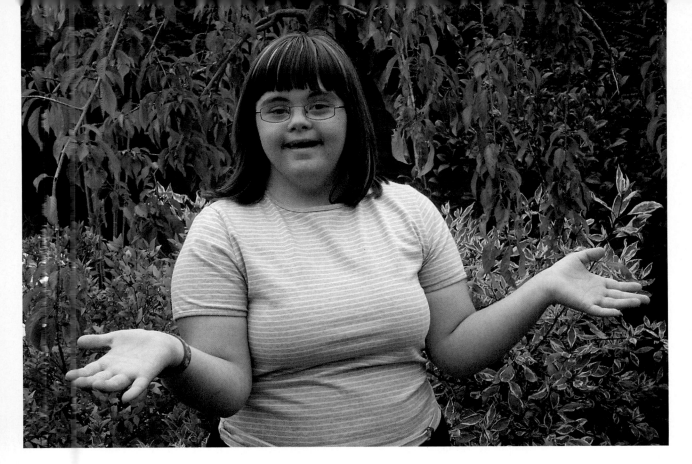

▲ This girl looks happy and confident about herself and her life.

would achieve nothing and they were encouraged to send them to special schools for people with learning difficulties. People believed they were not capable of thinking for themselves or making decisions about their own lives. Many people with Down syndrome lived at home with their parents with little or no support.

Changes

In the last 30 to 40 years, the attitude towards people with disabilities has changed, particularly in the more developed countries of Europe, North America, and Australia. Instead of seeing only the disability, people are encouraged to see the person as an individual who happens to have a disability. People with disabilities have the same rights to education and social care as everybody else. Children with Down syndrome often learn by copying other children, so they learn more

quickly in a mainstream school. Children with and without a disability can benefit greatly from being at school together. They can support each other and learn from each other. It helps them to accept and understand that everyone is different and has different needs. It also increases understanding of disabilities and helps to reduce prejudice.

JOHN LANGDON DOWN

Down syndrome is named after John Langdon Down, the doctor who in 1862 first noticed that some people in special schools shared several distinctive characteristics. He stated that ". . . In all these patients one is able to trace a marked physiological and psychological agreement. So much do they resemble one another that they might readily be taken for members of the same family."

Who has Down Syndrome?

Anyone can be born with Down syndrome. The condition occurs all over the world in every community and group of people. Down syndrome is caused by a genetic "accident" around the time of conception. It has nothing to do with anything the parents did or did not do. The only factor that makes it more likely to occur is the age of the mother.

Incidence of Down Syndrome

As far as it is possible to tell, people have always been born with Down syndrome. Paintings from the 16th century show people who look as if they may have had Down syndrome. Today, Down syndrome is the most common genetic disorder and worldwide figures show that approximately one in every 1000 babies has Down syndrome.

According to an estimate made in 2006, about 5400 babies are born with Down syndrome each year in the USA.

▼ *This chart shows that older mothers are more likely to have a baby with Down syndrome.*

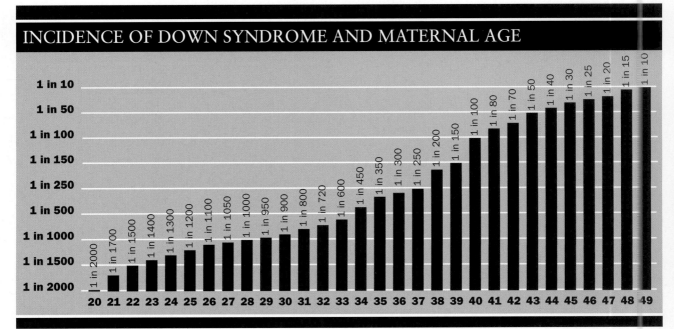

INCIDENCE OF DOWN SYNDROME AND MATERNAL AGE

Source: National Down Syndrome Society

◀ *Charles Darwin had ten children, the youngest of which is thought to have had Down syndrome.*

but it probably has something to do with the egg that the mother produces, or with the effect of aging on the mother.

Past Theories

In the past, people thought that the mother was responsible for giving birth to a baby with Down syndrome. They thought that sinful or immoral behavior or an addiction to alcohol were all possible causes. Alternatively, they thought that there must be something wrong with the mother's reproductive system or that the mother had been particularly stressed before the baby was conceived. All of these theories were found to be wrong in 1959 when the French scientist Dr. Jerome Lejeune discovered that the actual cause was an extra chromosome.

Age of Mother

The older the mother is when a baby is born, the more likely it is that the baby will have Down syndrome. However, most babies with Down syndrome are born to women under the age of 35, as younger women have more babies. The chances increase steadily with the increasing age of the mother, until they are one in every ten births for mothers who are older than 49 years. No one knows exactly why older mothers are more likely to give birth to babies with Down syndrome,

What are Chromosomes?

Your body is made up of trillions of tiny cells. Your bones are made of bone cells, your muscles of muscle cells, your kidneys of kidney cells, and so on. Most cells contain chromosomes that control what the cell does. Every cell usually has the same set of chromosomes.

Getting Started

Everyone's chromosomes are copied from their parents' chromosomes. Each sperm contains 23 chromosomes and each female egg has 23 similar chromosomes. When a sperm joins with an egg to make the first cell of a new baby, the 23 chromosomes from the father's sperm join the 23 chromosomes in the mother's egg to give 46 chromosomes, arranged in 23 matching pairs. This first cell then copies the chromosomes and divides into two cells. These two cells do the same to make four cells, and so on over and over again to form all the cells that make up the human body. Every new cell contains a complete set of 23 pairs.

Genes and DNA

Chromosomes are made up of strings of hundreds, and sometimes thousands, of genes. Altogether you have about 35,000 genes. Genes are made of chemical proteins called DNA. The DNA in your genes carries all the information that each cell needs to function. It also carries the inherited genetic information that decides much about the way you look and how well your body works.

▼ *Each cell has a nucleus, which contains the chromosomes. Chromosomes are made up of strands of genes which contain your unique DNA.*

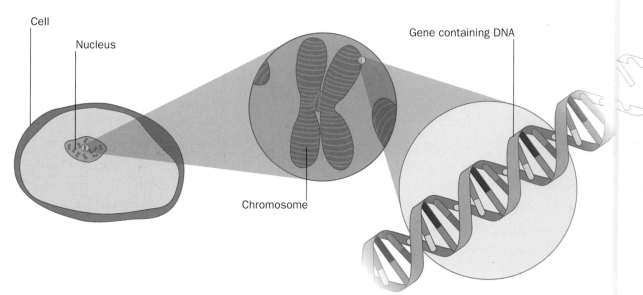

Cell

Nucleus

Gene containing DNA

Chromosome

Your DNA is unique to you. Only sets of multiples (like twins or triplets) start life with identical DNA. Your genes decide the color of your hair and the shape of your face, for example, and other things about your appearance. Some things about the way you look are due partly to inheritance and partly to how you interact with your environment. How tall you grow, for example, is decided mainly by your genes, but also by whether you eat a healthy diet when you are a child.

HUMAN GENOME PROJECT

All of your chromosomes, or your genetic material, is called your genome. Only 0.1 percent of genetic material varies to create the billions of different people in the world. The remaining 99.9 percent is identical in everyone. Scientists have now mapped the human genome and worked out the exact sequence of DNA in every gene. The National Human Genome Research Institute describes the project as "one of the great feats of exploration in history—an inward voyage of discovery rather than an outward exploration of the planet or the cosmos . . . Completed in April 2003, the [Human Genome Project] gave us the ability, for the first time, to read nature's complete genetic blueprint for building a human being."

▶ *Part of a molecule of DNA. It is shaped like a spiral ladder. Just four chemical bases (shown here in four colors) combine in different ways to make the "steps" of the ladder. The order of combinations determines the nature of the genes.*

The Extra Chromosome

Scientists have given the matching pairs of chromosomes numbers from one to 23. Some people have an extra chromosome in pair 21, so that they have three chromosomes 21 instead of two. This extra genetic material causes the physical characteristics and learning difficulties that people with Down syndrome have. The extra chromosome is either a random error that occurred when the sperm or egg formed, or an error that occurred as the embryo began to develop.

Trisomy 21

There are three types of Down syndrome. The most common form is free trisomy 21 in which every cell has an extra chromosome 21. It accounts for about 92 percent of people with Down syndrome. About three to four percent have translocation trisomy 21.

In this type of Down syndrome, the extra copy of chromosome 21 is attached to one of the other chromosomes. The effects of free trisomy and translocation trisomy are very similar.

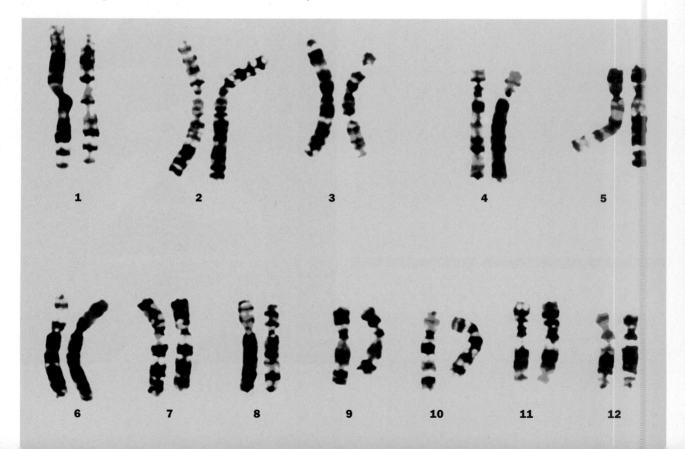

1

2

3

4

5

6

7

8

9

10

11

12

MELISSA'S STORY

"When people ask me what Down syndrome is, I tell them it's an extra chromosome. A doctor would tell you the extra chromosome causes an intellectual disability that makes it harder for me to learn things. (For instance, some of my classes are in a 'resource room,' where kids with many kinds of learning disabilities are taught at a different pace.)

When my mom first told me I had Down syndrome, I worried that people might think I wasn't as smart as they were, or that I talked or looked different. I just want to be like everyone else, so sometimes I wish I could give back the extra chromosome. But having Down syndrome is what makes me 'me.' And I'm proud of who I am. I'm a hard worker, a good person, and I care about my friends. I can't change that I have Down syndrome, but one thing I would change is how people think of me. I'd tell them: Judge me as a whole person, not just the person you see. Treat me with respect, and accept me for who I am. Most important, just be my friend. After all, I would do the same for you."

You can read more of Melissa's story on the National Geographic Kids web site.
http://kids.nationalgeographic.com/Stories/PeoplePlaces/Downsyndrome

Mosaicism

Mosaicism affects between two and four percent of people with Down syndrome. In this type, only some cells have the extra chromosome and only part of the extra chromosome may be present. People with mosaic Down syndrome may be physically less affected than people with free or translocation trisomy 21, but they usually have similar learning difficulties. There has been little research into the differences between mosaic Down syndrome and trisomy 21.

◀ ▼ *These are the chromosomes of a person with free trisomy 21. You can see that they have three chromosomes 21.*

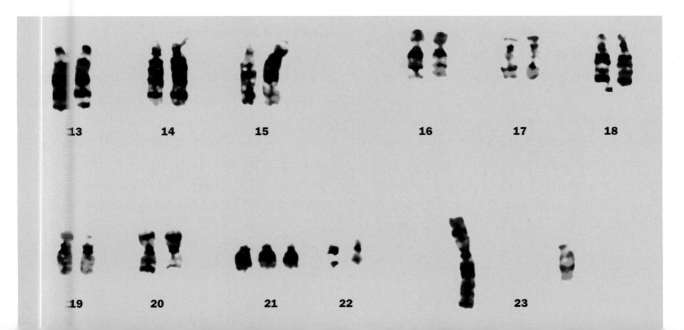

13   14   15   16   17   18

19   20   21   22   23

Individual Differences

Every person with Down syndrome is different. They may have some things in common, but each is an individual with unique looks and a unique personality. Some people with Down syndrome have severe learning difficulties while others have only mild learning difficulties. Not everybody has all the physical characteristics associated with the syndrome.

Physical Appearance

Like everyone else, people with Down syndrome look like their parents in many ways, but most also have particular features that are shared by other people with the condition. The most noticeable features are eyes that are wide-spaced and slanting, a small, flatter nose and shorter arms, legs, hands, feet, and toes. There are also other physical features that are less obvious, such as a short neck and a single crease on the palm of the hand.

Muscles and Joints

Almost all babies born with Down syndrome have poor muscle tone, a condition called hypotonia. This makes their muscles weaker than those of other babies. Fewer than five out of a hundred babies with Down syndrome have good muscle tone.

Hypotonia affects all of the muscles in the body including, for example, the muscles in the digestive system. Many babies with Down syndrome also have loose joints. Together, hypotonia and loose joints mean that babies with Down syndrome tend to be very floppy and inactive. As babies grow, their muscles become stronger. The process can be helped by special exercises that parents or caregivers can do with babies (see page 26).

Intellectual Impairment

The extra genetic material on chromosome 21 affects intellectual ability. Children with Down syndrome are slower at learning new information and new skills than most other children. Most co learn to talk, read, and write but take longer to do so. Even as adults, people with Down syndrome take longer to learn new skills.

Emotional Development

Children with Down syndrome develop more slowly emotionally as well as intellectually. They go through all the same stages as other children, but often later on. For example, a five or six-year old Down syndrome child may have the kind of tantrums that other children have when they are two years old. Children with Down syndrome will often understand far more than they are able to express. Those who find it hard to express

▲ *Everyone with Down syndrome looks different and has their own personality.*

themselves sometimes become angry or frustrated. People with Down syndrome share the same emotions as other people. They have the same hopes and fears and the same feelings, such as love, loneliness, and boredom.

Personality

In the past it was thought that people with Down syndrome had a particular kind of personality.

They were said to be loving and gentle, and to have a good sense of humor, but they could be stubborn. John Langdon Down said, "No amount of coercion (force) will induce (persuade) them to do that which they have made up their minds not to do." This, however, is true of many people. Today it is understood that people with Down syndrome each have their own personality and that they are very different from one another.

Health Problems

People with Down syndrome often have health problems caused by their extra genetic material. Their immune systems are sometimes weak, so they are more likely to catch illnesses, such as colds, and they often have runny noses. They may also have problems with their heart, eyesight, and hearing, and some have diabetes.

Some people with the condition may have several medical problems, while others have only a few, and some have none at all.

Heart Problems

About 50 percent of babies with Down syndrome have heart problems. Sometimes the problem is minor and disappears without treatment. About seven out of every hundred babies have severe heart problems that need to be operated on in the first few months of the baby's life. The most common heart problem is a hole in the heart. If the hole is in the center of the heart, the baby will need to be operated on, but if the hole is small and between the two halves of the heart, it may heal on its own.

Ears and Eyes

In 1999, an Australian study found that more than three-quarters of children with Down syndrome have problems with sight, including squints, farsightedness and nearsightedness, and more than half have hearing problems. Some children with Down syndrome need a hearing aid, but most

▶ *Children with Down syndrome are five times more likely to wear glasses than other children.*

children with hearing difficulties have "glue ear," which means that thick mucus behind the eardrum stops sound waves from passing through the ear. The condition can be corrected by draining the mucus away and inserting small tubes to keep the ears clear. The hearing problems that some children with Down syndrome have may continue into adulthood.

Diabetes

About one in every 250 children with Down syndrome has diabetes, making it seven times more common than in other children. Diabetes occurs when the body does not produce enough insulin to control blood glucose levels, so they can become too high or too low. Symptoms of diabetes include tiredness, extreme thirst, and a frequent need to pass urine. The condition can be treated with a low-sugar diet and injections of insulin.

▼ *The heart pumps blood to the lungs and then around the body.*

HOW THE HEART WORKS

The heart has four chambers and is a double pump. The two chambers on the left side of the heart receive blood from the body and pump it to the lungs. Here the blood takes in fresh supplies of oxygen and gets rid of carbon dioxide. The blood then returns to the right side of the heart, from where it is pumped around the body. If a baby has a hole in the heart, some of the blood from the left side can move into the right side without going to the lungs first. This means that the body receives blood that is low in oxygen.

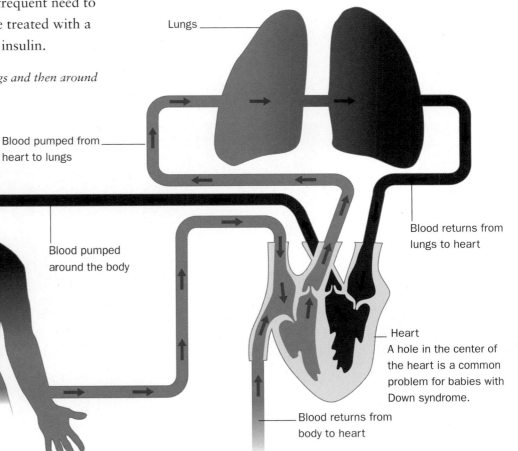

Lungs

Blood pumped from heart to lungs

Blood returns from lungs to heart

Heart

Lungs

Blood pumped around the body

Heart
A hole in the center of the heart is a common problem for babies with Down syndrome.

Blood returns from body to heart

Testing for Down Syndrome

Tests for Down syndrome can be done very early, even before the baby is born. In some countries, pregnant women are offered screening tests to predict the possibility that the baby may have Down syndrome.

Screening Tests

The simplest screening test involves taking a sample of the mother's blood. It is examined for the presence of various hormones and proteins, which have entered the mother's blood from the fetus. Screening tests are usually done between the 10th and 18th week of the pregnancy. They are easy to do and do not put the baby at risk.

▼ *A nurse performs an ultrasound scan. The computer screen shows a picture of the unborn baby in the womb.*

An ultrasound is another way of screening for Down syndrome. An ultrasound scan creates a moving picture of the fetus on a computer. Studies suggest that certain factors (known as markers) seen on a scan may give an indication of Down syndrome. A skilled operator will be able to see if there are any defects in the heart, kidneys, or digestive system, for example, all of which are more common in babies with Down syndrome than other babies.

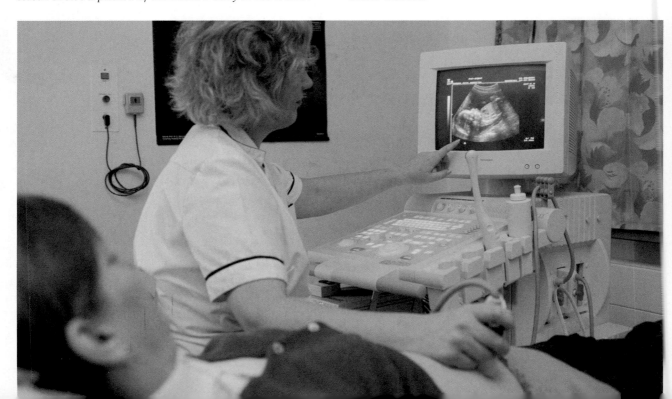

Interpreting the Screening Tests

The screening tests only give a likelihood of the presence of Down syndrome. Many women who appear to have a high risk of having a baby with Down syndrome will turn out not to be carrying a baby with Down syndrome, while others who appear to have a very low risk may actually have a baby with Down syndrome. If there is a greater than one in 250 chance that a baby has Down syndrome, the mother will be offered a diagnostic test which will give her a more reliable result.

Diagnostic Tests

The placenta, umbilical cord, and amniotic fluid are produced by the fetus in the earliest days of the pregnancy. This means that they have the same genes as the fetus, and not the genes of the mother. Diagnostic tests take either a small sample of the amniotic fluid, a small sample of the placenta or a sample of the umbilical cord. With each test there is a slight risk that the mother will miscarry.

If the diagnostic test shows an extra chromosome 21 the parents might be offered the option to terminate the pregnancy. This is always a difficult decision for parents to make. Parents should be given information by doctors about Down syndrome so that they can make a reasoned decision. Diagnostic tests can only tell you whether or not a baby has Down syndrome, they cannot tell exactly how a child will be affected.

▶ *A needle is used to collect a small sample of the amniotic fluid in the womb during a diagnostic test.*

SAFE CAPSULE

Inside the womb, the fetus floats in amniotic fluid, which protects it from being knocked or squashed. The umbilical cord connects the fetus to the placenta. This is a spongy mass into which blood from the mother and the fetus flow. Here the fetus's blood picks up oxygen and food and gets rid of waste.

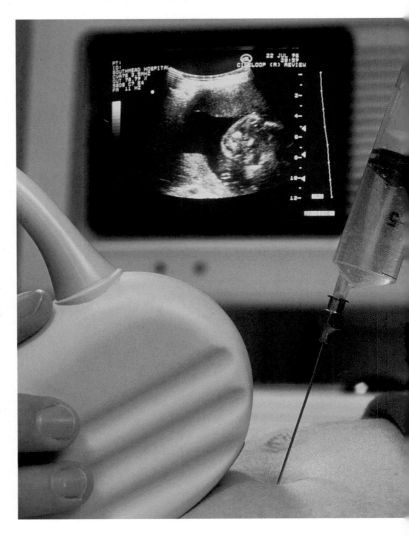

Diagnosing at Birth

Despite prenatal screening and testing, most cases of Down syndrome are diagnosed soon after birth. This will not be a surprise for parents who had a positive diagnostic test before their baby was born, but for other parents it may come as a shock.

Immediate Signs

Midwives and pediatricians can quickly tell if a newborn baby has Down syndrome. Although all babies are born with weak neck and back muscles, babies with Down syndrome are often particularly limp. They may also show other signs of the condition, such as the distinctive shaped eyes or a single crease on the palm of their hand. A blood sample is taken from the baby to make a definite diagnosis.

Hearing the News

Parents who were expecting to have a typical baby are often very upset and angry when they first learn that their baby has Down syndrome. Finding out your child is disabled can be like planning a vacation to Hawaii and finding yourself in Ohio: "Ohio?!?" you might think. "What do you mean, Ohio?? I signed up for Hawaii! I'm supposed to be in Hawaii. All my life I've dreamed of going to Hawaii." Once parents find out more about Down

► *Health visitors and other professionals are ready to help mothers whose babies have Down syndrome. They can give lots of advice to new mothers on the care their new baby will need.*

▲ *All newborn babies cry as soon as they start breathing. Babies with Down syndrome often cry for shorter periods or may not cry at all.*

syndrome and bond with their new baby, however, they come to realize that "Ohio" is simply a different place. Their baby will still become a well loved member of their family.

SARA'S STORY

"We welcomed our ball of energy, Kaleb Jonathan, to the world on July 29, 2002. From the get-go he was ready to conquer the world. You can imagine our surprise when we went for Kaleb's two week checkup and he was diagnosed with Down syndrome. I was in shock. I could not imagine that this was happening to us.

I was 22 years old: didn't this only happen to older mothers? (To which, by the way, the answer is a big NO!) We felt like this was something that happened only to other people. We certainly shed some tears and learned that crying is OK. We were terrified of all of the problems the doctor told us often come along with DS—such as heart problems . . . It was so much to hear all at once. Luckily, Kaleb's heart is fine. It had a small hole that closed up within a year, which is very common.

Kaleb is progressing wonderfully. He does have to wear glasses for farsightedness and has a slightly crossed eye, but, if that's the least of our worries right now, we're happy! We may have struggles still to come down the road, but we don't worry about them constantly like I thought we would. Instead we are content with all of the things that he DOES do now. I would not change one second of my life with him. He has taught me patience, understanding, forgiveness and most importantly, unconditional love."

Babies with Down Syndrome

Babies with Down syndrome may be different from other babies in several ways. Their weaker muscles can make it more difficult for them to suck milk and they can be slow to move their heads, arms, and legs. There are many things that parents and caregivers can do to help a baby with Down syndrome.

Feeding

Feeding a baby with Down syndrome often takes longer than with other babies. This is because most babies with Down syndrome suck weakly and feed slowly. Their lips may not grip the nipple of the bottle tightly enough, and they may fall asleep before they have had enough milk. Parents have to be patient and keep encouraging the baby to feed. Some babies with Down syndrome cry less loudly and for a shorter length of time than other babies. Some babies with the condition hardly cry at all, and may need to be woken for a feeding.

Moving

Babies begin to move from the moment they are born. Babies with Down syndrome, however, are less inclined to move. Parents can encourage their babies to move by handling them a lot—cuddling them, hugging them, and massaging them. As the weeks pass, the people who care for the baby should encourage them to turn their heads, stretch their arms and legs, and eventually roll over.

▲ *Playing with a baby strengthens the baby's muscles and helps him or her to develop socially.*

▲ *This baby can lift her head and shoulders. She is halfway to being able to crawl.*

Encouraging a Baby to Move

You can encourage a baby to turn their head by, for example, tickling their ear, or making a sound behind their head. Putting a toy just out of their reach encourages the baby to move their hands and arms. The baby can be gently rolled over and should be frequently carried around. The tongue is a muscle, too. Babies with Down syndrome often have difficulty controlling their tongue. Parents can help their baby develop better tongue control by making faces for the baby to imitate and, as they get older, encouraging them to make noises.

BACK MUSCLES

All babies are born with weak neck and back muscles. At first, all babies need to have their heads supported. As their neck muscles become stronger, babies can hold up their own heads. When babies are a few months old, their muscles become strong enough for them to roll over. As the back muscles continue to strengthen, babies are able to sit up and then to stand up. Babies with Down syndrome go through the same process, but it usually takes much longer for their muscles to strengthen.

Toddlers with Down Syndrome

Toddlers are very busy. They learn to crawl and walk, and they learn to talk.

Infants with Down syndrome usually take longer to learn these things.

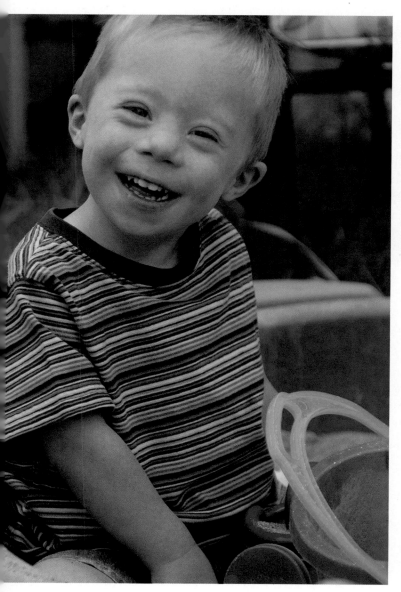

All babies learn to do things at their own pace, but most babies begin to walk when they are about a year old. They begin to say words at around the same time, and most can talk by about two years of age. The average toddler with Down syndrome does not learn to walk until they are two years old or more. A child with Down syndrome may be five or six years old before they can talk well enough to express themselves.

Walking

Hypotonia and loose joints both play a part in adding to the length of time it takes for a toddler with Down syndrome to learn to walk. Both conditions make it harder for the child's legs to carry his or her weight. Finding their balance is difficult because it requires good, strong stomach muscles. Special exercises can help to strengthen a toddler's muscles and joints. The exercises will not help them to walk any sooner, but they will eventually help them to walk better.

◀ *A toddler with Down syndrome plays in a sandbox. Playing with sand helps toddlers to develop coordination between their muscles and their eyes.*

▶ *This little girl has managed to pull herself up so that she can stand by herself.*

Talking

Children with Down syndrome usually take a long time to learn to talk. They find it difficult to say words clearly, partly because the muscles in their face, lips and tongue are weak, and partly because many have hearing problems—if a child cannot hear words clearly, it is hard to speak them clearly.

The main reason for problems with speech, however, is that it is difficult for children with Down syndrome to learn how language works. Even when they are older, many children and adults with Down syndrome have difficulty talking and saying words clearly. Friends and family who know them well can understand what they are saying, but if you meet somebody for the first time it may take a while to tune in to their way of communicating. There are many forms of communication and people with Down syndrome are often very good at finding ways to make themselves understood.

Signing

Being unable to communicate well is very frustrating for children with Down syndrome. Talking, however, is not the only way to get your message across. Most families use signing with their toddlers with Down syndrome to help them communicate more easily. Signing acts as a bridge to speaking and it can help to increase a child's vocabulary when they do begin to talk.

At School

Children with Down syndrome vary considerably in how much and how quickly they can learn. Some children with the condition may not learn to read or write, but others may have an Individual Education Plan (IEP) or take special education courses. Any child with Down syndrome can graduate from high school.

It is important that children with Down syndrome go to a school that is right for them. Some children with Down syndrome may do much better in a special school, but most children with Down syndrome learn best in a mainstream school alongside other children.

Intellectual Differences

Children with Down syndrome have particular difficulties with learning. Their short-term memory is poor and they find it hard to concentrate for long periods of time. Their fine motor skills are poor, which means that they find it difficult to control small movements, such as those needed for writing. They also find it hard to do two things at once. Children with Down syndrome have good visual skills, so they learn best when they can see how something works, and they learn fastest when new things are broken down into small stages.

▼ *Most children with Down syndrome fit in well with—and learn best in—a mixed class in a public school.*

CASE NOTES

FRASER'S STORY

Fraser is five years old, lives in Australia and has Down syndrome. His mother, Fiona, prepared notes for his teachers before he started school. Here, she explains how Fraser can understand more words than he is able to speak:

"Fraser's capacity to understand is far more advanced than his expressive language. As a result there is a risk of underestimating how much he can understand. That being said, however, he does have trouble understanding complex commands. And will avoid talking if at all possible. Why? Essentially because speaking is hard work, both cognitively and physically —but if he is praised for his efforts his eyes light up and he blossoms. He can use four-word sentences. For example—I like the Simpsons. But he will say this only if prompted."

Public Schools

Having a child with Down syndrome in the classroom can be good for the whole class: it helps children to be more aware and accepting of human diversity and individuality. The teaching methods that work best for children with Down syndrome, such as practical hands-on experience and visual explanations, also work well with other children. A child with Down syndrome will need extra help in the classroom, however.

▼ *This student with Down syndrome is getting extra help with the class lesson.*

Friendships and Fun

People with Down syndrome enjoy the same activities as other people. They may like listening to music, watching television and DVDs, and going to the movies. Many enjoy swimming, horse-riding, gymnastics, and other sports.

▲ *Special clubs provide an opportunity for young people with a disability to meet each other and make friends.*

▲ *An athlete competes in the Special Olympics European Youth Games in Rome, Italy. The Youth Games involves 1,400 intellectually disabled athletes from all 55 Special Olympics National Programs in the region.*

Clubs

As well as joining mainstream clubs, where they can mix with children without disabilities, children with Down syndrome often join special clubs for children with different kinds of disabilities. Many special clubs are organized and situated locally. They offer a chance for people to get together, have fun, talk about their interests, and discuss things that are important to them. They may organize outings and vacations, too. Other clubs are organized around a particular sport, such as horse-riding, or provide a wide range of sports. The club Special Olympics, for example, offers many different sports and training to people with learning difficulties. Now there are also many online clubs that people can join, which connect people with Down syndrome around the world.

JOSEPH'S STORY

Joseph is 19 years old and has Down syndrome. He has taken part in many sports since he was very young. This is what he says about sports and other activities that he enjoys:

"Swimming is good. I'm good at it. I like diving in and relays. I swim about 5 times a week and my best mate is my coach John. I like winning medals at galas. I swam in Rome in 2006 at the Special Olympics European Youth Games and won 1 gold and 2 silvers. I've swam in Scotland, Wales, and different places in England and I'm in the DSISO* GB Squad.

In 2008 I won 2 medals in Pila, Italy at the Special Olympics GB Winter Games doing skiing. I go to Magpie Dance and learn technique and dance and I'm doing an Arts Award at Corali Dance. I play snooker [a game similar to pool] and I love football [soccer]. Chelsea is the best! I go to Cyberzone Computer Club and I play football at Friday Friends. I go on trips with my school and with my youth club. I went to athletics but now I do dance instead.

I like watching *James Bond, Harry Potter, Pink Panther, Fawlty Towers,* and *EastEnders.*

My girlfriend is Hannah. She's a lovely girl. We do sports and dance together."

* DSISO – Down Syndrome International Swimming Organization

Effects on the Family

While special exercises help a child with Down syndrome to develop to their full potential, the child benefits most from being a member of a happy, loving, and active family that does all the things that families normally do.

Family Life

Looking after a baby or child with Down syndrome can be more demanding and time-consuming than looking after other children. A baby with Down syndrome may need more appointments with doctors and therapists than other children. It is important for parents to find a balance between the needs of the child with Down syndrome and the rest of the family. After getting over the shock of hearing that a baby has Down syndrome, most families have very normal lives.

▼ *This happy family photo includes grandparents, parents, and two children.*

▲ *Alexandra, Victoria's younger sister.*

Siblings

Brothers and sisters need to learn what Down syndrome is and how it will affect their sibling. They may, at times, resent the fact that more attention is given to the child with Down syndrome, and may not understand the reasons for this until they are older. Nevertheless, brothers and sisters of children with Down syndrome often learn to be caring and helpful. They usually help their parents around the house, and may learn to be more independent and tolerant than other children of their age.

CASE NOTES

VICTORIA'S STORY

Victoria is 27 years old. Her sister Alexandra is 20 months younger and has Down syndrome.

"Having a sister with Down Syndrome has been a bag of mixed emotions for me. When I was younger Alex was 'just my sister,' but when I was about nine I realized we weren't the same as other families. A girl at Guides was picking on Alex—but through me—and kept it up week after week, which really upset me. I felt angry with her, but also angry that I couldn't tell my parents because it would upset them. I remember people always looking and staring in the street, which used to annoy me. I thought, 'I wish it was all different to this and we were normal.'

Now I can see that people are in the wrong to stare and it's their problem as they are probably uneducated about Down. Now I feel angry that people may stare at Alex and I'm not there to protect her.

I am so proud of Alex and how well she has done. I enjoy shopping with Alex and love buying her new clothes so that she feels good about herself. I hate seeing young people with Down wearing ill-fitting cast-offs as they deserve to be dressed fashionably like other young people. I am amazed that Alex is able to hold down two jobs, use public transport, and will soon leave home being able to do all the household jobs that I do. It still makes me sad that she may never have all the life experiences that I have but I am happy to support her and help her gain more happiness in her life."

Living Independently

People with Down syndrome continue to develop and learn new things throughout their adult life. As they grow up they, like other young adults, want to live more independent lives, get a job, have relationships, and leave home. Most people with Down syndrome, however, can only do these things with support.

Work

There are various options for people with Down syndrome when they leave school. They may attend day centers or college, and they may work in supported employment. This includes jobs in ordinary companies where the person with a disability has support to help them do their job. They may have a support worker to help them get to and from their job and they may have extra help within the company, particularly when learning how to do the job. Many people with Down syndrome attend day centers or college for part of the week and also work part-time like many other young adults.

▼ *This young man, who works in a bakery, happens to have Down syndrome.*

Another possibility is volunteer work. Alexandra (see page 35), for example, studied catering at college and then got a job working in a Christian coffee shop. After the coffee shop closed down, she worked as a volunteer in a community center run by the Salvation Army.

Living

Some adults with Down syndrome continue to live at home or with a member of their family. Others move out of home into group homes. Here they are given different levels of support depending on their individual needs. Some people with Down syndrome live almost completely independently, shopping and cooking for themselves. Provided they are helped and supported, either by their families or by social services, people with Down syndrome can live the same kind of life as everybody else.

▲ *Being in love is an important part of most people's lives. This young couple enjoy life together.*

EQUAL OPPORTUNITIES

Many countries have laws that guarantee equal opportunities for people with disabilities. In the United States, the 1990 Americans with Disabilities Act prohibits employers from discriminating against people with disabilities, provided they are qualified for the job. In the United Kingdom, the 1999 Disability Rights Commission Act stops discrimination against disabled people at work, in education, in transport, and in shops. The Act is now part of the British Equality and Human Rights Commission.

The Future

Although much is already known about Down syndrome, researchers are discovering new information all the time. This new knowledge helps us to understand better how people with Down syndrome can be supported in today's world.

Research

Much research focuses on understanding the difficulties that people with Down syndrome have in learning and how they learn best. For example, research in the last 30 years has shown that people with Down syndrome learn best when they are taught visually—when they can picture what they are learning, rather than listening to an explanation. As a result of research, people with Down syndrome are now better educated and so able to live fuller lives.

The Human Genome Project (see page 15) has successfully conducted some research into chromosome 21. It is hoped that future research will bring a greater understanding of the development of people with Down syndrome and why there is a higher incidence of certain medical problems in people with Down syndrome.

▼ *With family support, children with Down syndrome can grow up to be happy, confident members of society.*

▶ People with Down syndrome are now living longer thanks to a better understanding of their condition, and the improvements in medical treatment.

Further research may help us to learn more about why having Down syndrome is in some instances an advantage. People with Down syndrome do not seem to get certain types of cancer, and multiple sclerosis is almost unknown. When they get older, some people with Down syndrome have all the signs of Alzheimer's disease in their brains, but they do not actually have Alzheimer's disease. Scientists want to find out what it is that protects people with Down syndrome against certain illnesses. Maybe people with Down syndrome will prove to be the key to helping find answers about why some illnesses happen, and this information may help us to understand how we can cure certain illnesses. Perhaps our society may finally begin to honor and respect people with Down syndrome because of what they can and do contribute to society.

Down Syndrome Community

Many organizations have been set up to provide information about Down syndrome and to support families and people with Down syndrome. Most have several functions, which may include giving help and advice to the families of those with Down syndrome, giving care and support to those with Down syndrome, fundraising through events and sponsorship, raising awareness and campaigning for the rights of those with Down syndrome.
Worldwide bodies are much larger and organize conferences to discuss areas of research and share ideas. It is this network of organizations that makes the Down syndrome community so strong.

"In the past, it was believed that there were many things that people with Down syndrome could not do, when in fact they had never been given the opportunity to try. Now, people with Down syndrome break boundaries every day by taking on and succeeding with new challenges both small and large." Down Syndrome Association, UK

SPECIAL DIETS AND SUPPLEMENTS

Although there is no cure for Down syndrome, many parents of children with Down syndrome are turning to herbal remedies and other forms of alternative medicine. However, Sue Buckley of the Down Syndrome Educational Trust, a charity involved with education and research into Down syndrome, says that "At present there are no known pharmacological or 'nutritional' treatments that have been shown to have any effect on the developmental progress of children with Down syndrome."

Glossary

alternative medicine forms of medicine that are different from those traditionally taught in universities and practiced by GPs and hospitals

amniotic fluid the fluid that surrounds an unborn baby in the womb

autism a disorder in which a person has difficulties with communication and understanding others and their emotions

cerebral palsy a term used to describe a range of difficulties, mainly affecting movement, that are caused by brain damage

chromosome a tiny strand of genes, made up of DNA, found in each cell

cognitively in a way that uses thought and knowledge

conception when a male sperm joins with a female egg to create the first cell of a new baby

day center a place that provides care and activities for people who are not completely independent

diabetes a condition in which a person has too much glucose in their blood because their body does not produce enough of the hormone insulin

diagnose to identify a disease or condition after careful examination of the body and symptoms

diagnostic test a test that provides evidence that shows whether or not a person has a particular condition or disease

discriminate to treat differently on the basis of prejudice

distinctive special, relating only to a particular set of circumstances

DNA chemicals that combine to form genes. DNA contains the coded instructions that tell each living cell what to do

embryo fetus that is still developing

equal opportunities having the same possibility of education and work as other people

expressive language words that convey meaning

farsightedness the ability to see things more clearly if they are far away

fetus a baby before it is born

gene the basic unit of heredity by which characteristics are passed from one generation to the next

genetic condition a medical problem caused by a fault in the genes

genome all the chromosomes in the cell of a particular type, or species, of life

glucose a type of sugar found in food that is turned into energy inside the body

hormone a chemical made by one part of your body that causes a change or reaction in another part of your body

hypotonia less tone or tension in the muscles than normal

immune system mechanisms that protect the body from germs and diseases

inheritance the process of passing on physical characteristics from parents to their offspring

insulin the hormone produced by the pancreas that helps the body to convert glucose into energy

miscarry to give birth to an embryo or fetus before it is able to live

mosaicism a form of Down syndrome in which only some cells carry extra genetic material from chromosome 21

motor skills ability to do tasks that use muscles, such as throwing a ball or writing

mucus thick, slimy liquid that moistens and protects organs' surfaces inside the body

multiple sclerosis a disease where the body's immune system attacks its own nerve cells. It may cause problems with speech, vision, movement and bladder function

nearsightedness the ability to see things more clearly if they are close by

nutritional having to do with food

pediatric consultant a doctor who specializes in treating babies and children

pharmacological to do with drugs

physiological to do with the way the body works

placenta the organ in the womb that allows substances to pass between the mother's blood and the unborn baby's blood

prenatal before birth

protein a complex chemical that is part of living things and which living things need to take in from food

psychological to do with the mind

reproductive system parts of the body involved in producing new life

screening test a test designed to show whether a person has a particular disease or condition

sperm the male reproductive cell

symptoms changes in the body that indicate that a disease or other condition is present

termination deliberate ending

translocation when a chromosome or part of a chromosome becomes attached to another chromosome

trisomy 21 the medical name for Down syndrome —it indicates that there are three chromosomes 21

ultrasound a way of forming a picture of part of the inside of the body using sound waves

umbilical cord the tube that joins an unborn baby to the placenta

voluntary work unpaid work that someone chooses to do to help others

womb an organ in the lower body of a woman where babies grow and develop

Further Information

Books

Count Us In: Growing Up With Down Syndrome
Jason Kingsley and Mitchell Levitz, *Harcourt*, 2007

Down Syndrome (Genetic Diseases and Disorders)
Phillip Margulies, *Rosen Publishing Group*, 2007

Down Syndrome (Health Alert)
Marlene Targ Brill, *Benchmark Books*, 2006

Fasten Your Seatbelt: A Crash Course on Down Syndrome for Brothers and Sisters
Brian Skotko and Susan Levine, *Woodbine House*, 2009

Kellie's Book: The Art of the Possible
Kellie Greenwald, *Rayve Productions*, 2008

Living with Down Syndrome
Jenny Bryan, *Hodder Wayland*, 2006

Matthew: A Memoir
Anne Crosby, **Paul Dry Books**, 2006

My Friend has Down Syndrome
Jennifer Moore-Mallinos, *Barrons Educationa Series, Inc.*, 2008

My Name Is Not Slow: Youth with Mental Retardation
Autumn Libal, *Mason Crest Publishers Inc.*, 2004

The Year My Son and I Were Born
Kathryn Lynard Soper, *GPP Life*, 2009

Organizations

Canadian Down Syndrome Society
1-800-883-5608
www.cdss.ca

Down Syndrome Research Foundation
1-888-464-DSRF
www.dsrf.org

Down Syndrome Research Foundation & Resource
Center
1-888-464-DSRF
www.dsrf.org

International Mosaic Down Syndrome Association
1-888-MDS-LINK
www.imdsa.org

National Association for Down Syndrome [NADS]
630-325-9112
www.nads.org

National Down Syndrome Congress
1-800-232-NDSC
www.ndsccenter.org

National Down Syndrome Society
1-800-221-4602
www.ndss.org

Web Sites

International Down Syndrome Group:
A Social Networking Site
http://intdownsorg.ning.com

The Down Syndrome Web Ring
http://s.webring.com/hub?ring=downsyn

The Special Olympics
www.specialolympics.org

Note to Parents and Teachers: Every effort has been made by the publishers to ensure that these web sites are suitable for children, that they are of the highest educational value, and that they contain no inappropriate or offensive material. However, because of the nature of the Internet, it is impossible to guarantee that the contents of these sites will not be altered. We strongly advise that Internet access is supervised by a responsible adult.

Index

Titles and Contents in Explaining . . .

Explaining Asthma

What is Asthma? • History of Asthma • Increase in Asthma • Who has Asthma? • Healthy Lungs • How Asthma Affects the Lungs • What Triggers Asthma? • Asthma and Allergies • Diagnosing Asthma • Preventing an Attack • Relieving an Attack • What to Do During an Attack • Growing Up with Asthma • Living with Asthma • Asthma and Exercise • Asthma Treatments

Explaining Autism

What is Autism? • Autism: A Brief History • The Rise of Autism • The Autistic Spectrum • The Signs of Autism • Autism and Inheritance • The Triggers of Autism • Autism and the Body • Autism and Mental Health • Can Autism Be Treated? • Living with Autism • Autism and Families • Autism and School • Asperger Syndrome • Autism and Adulthood • The Future for Autism

Explaining Blindness

What is Blindness? • Causes and Effects • Visual Impairment • Color Blindness and Night Blindness • Eye Tests • Treatments and Cures • Coping with Blindness • Optical Aids • On the Move • Guide Dogs and Canes • Home Life • Blindness and Families • Blindness at School • Blindness as an Adult • Blindness, Sports, and Leisure • The Future for Blindness

Explaining Cerebral Palsy

What is Cerebral Palsy? • The Causes of Cerebral Palsy • Diagnosis • Types of Cerebral Palsy • Other Effects of Cerebral Palsy • Managing Cerebral Palsy • Other Support • Technological Support • Communication • How It Feels • Everyday Life • Being at School • Cerebral Palsy and the Family • Into Adulthood • Raising Awareness • The Future

Explaining Cystic Fibrosis

What is Cystic Fibrosis? • Cystic Fibrosis: A Brief History • What Causes Cystic Fibrosis? • Screening and Diagnosis • The Effects of Cystic Fibrosis • How is Cystic Fibrosis Managed? • Infections and Illness • A Special Diet • Clearing the Airways • Physical Exercise • Cystic Fibrosis and Families • Cystic Fibrosis at School • Growing Up with Cystic Fibrosis • New Treatments • The Future

Explaining Deafness

What is Deafness? • Ears and Sounds • Types of Deafness • Causes of Deafness • Signs of Deafness • Diagnosis • Treating Deafness • Lip Reading • Sign Language • Deafness and Education • Schools for the Deaf • Deafness and Adulthood • Technology • Deafness and the Family • Fighting Discrimination • The Future for Deafness

Explaining Diabetes

What is Diabetes? • Diabetes: A Brief History • Type 1 Diabetes • Type 2 Diabetes • Symptoms and Diagnosis • Medication • Hypoglycemia • Eyes, Skin, and Feet • Other Health Issues • Healthy Eating and Drinking • Physical Activity • Living with Diabetes • Diabetes and Families • Diabetes at School • Growing Up with Diabetes • Diabetes Treatment

Explaining Down Syndrome

What is Down Syndrome? • Changing Attitudes • Who has Down Syndrome? • What are Chromosomes? • The Extra Chromosome • Individual Differences • Health Problems • Testing for Down Syndrome • Diagnosing at Birth • Babies with Down Syndrome • Toddlers with Down Syndrome • At School • Friendships and Fun • Effects on the Family • Living Independently • The Future

Explaining Epilepsy

What is Epilepsy? • Causes and Effects • Who has Epilepsy? • Partial Seizures • Generalized Seizures • Triggers • Diagnosis • How You Can Help • Controlling Epilepsy • Taking Medicines • Living with Epilepsy • Epilepsy and Families • Epilepsy at School • Sports and Leisure • Growing Up with Epilepsy • Epilepsy Treatments

Explaining Food Allergies

What are Food Allergies? • Food Allergies: A Brief History • Food Aversion, Intolerance, or Allergy? • What Is an Allergic Reaction? • Food Allergies: Common Culprits • Anaphylaxis • Testing for Food Allergies • Avoiding Allergic Reactions • Treating Allergic Reactions • Food Allergies on the Rise • Food Allergies and Families • Food Allergies and Age • Living with Food Allergies • 21st Century Problems • Treatment for Food Allergies